Elven Beauties

Adult Coloring Book

Fashion Sketchbook Collection

S. Parks

Thank you for buying this first edition of Fashion Sketchbook Series; a coloring book collection of hand-drawn illustrations by Stephen A. Parks.

Dedications

Thanks to my wife, Jennifer, for helping with the inking of the illustrations. I could never have done this without you!

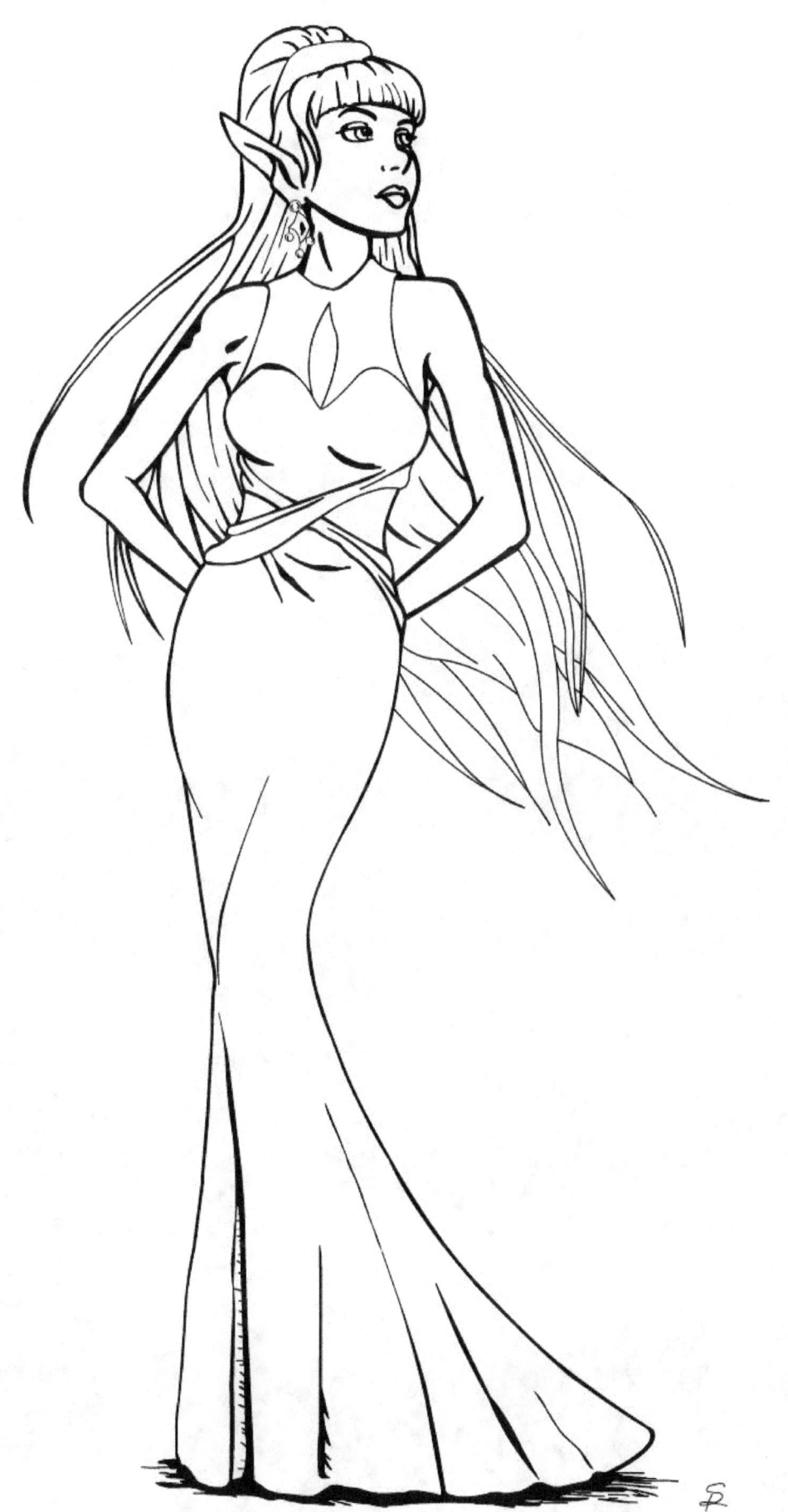

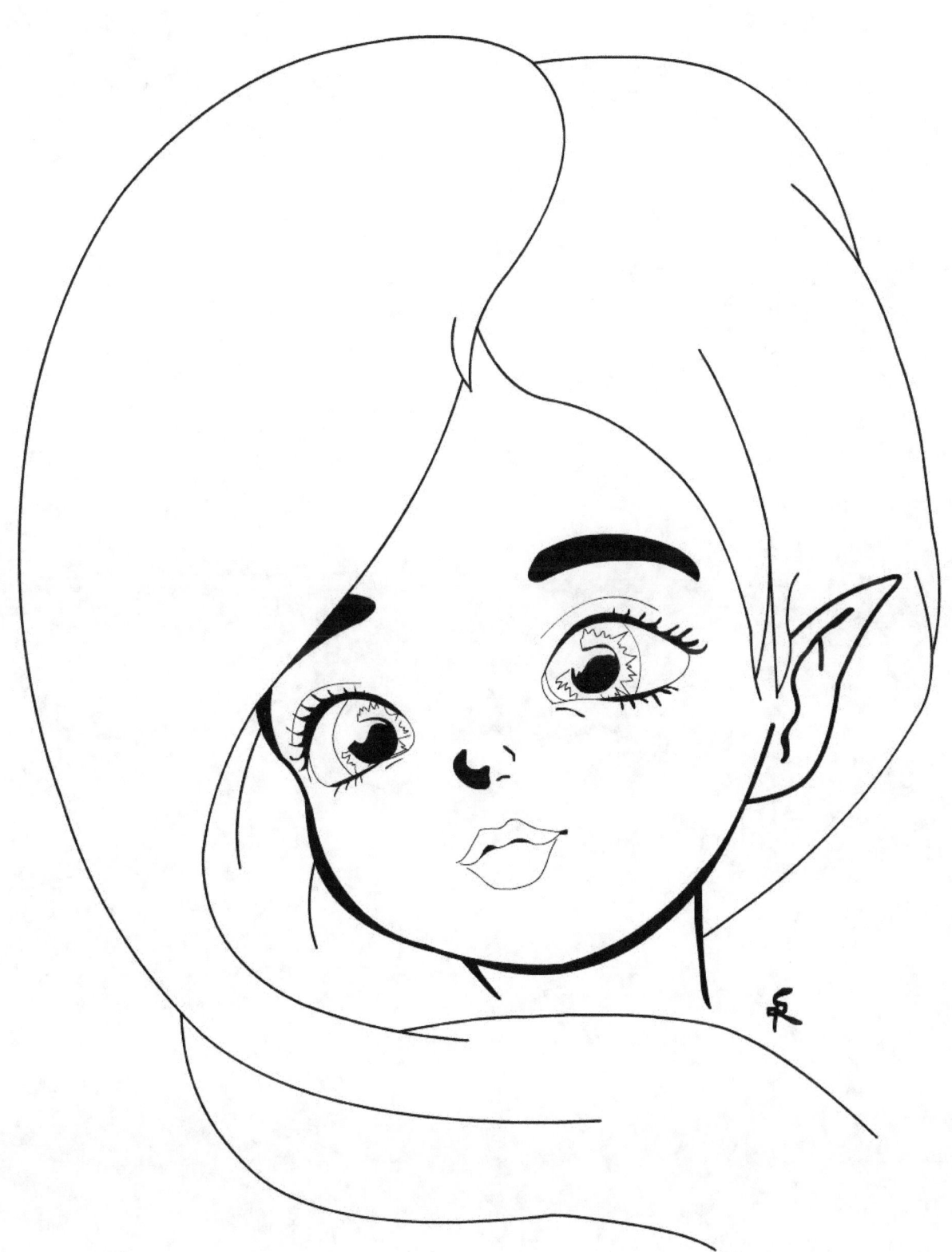

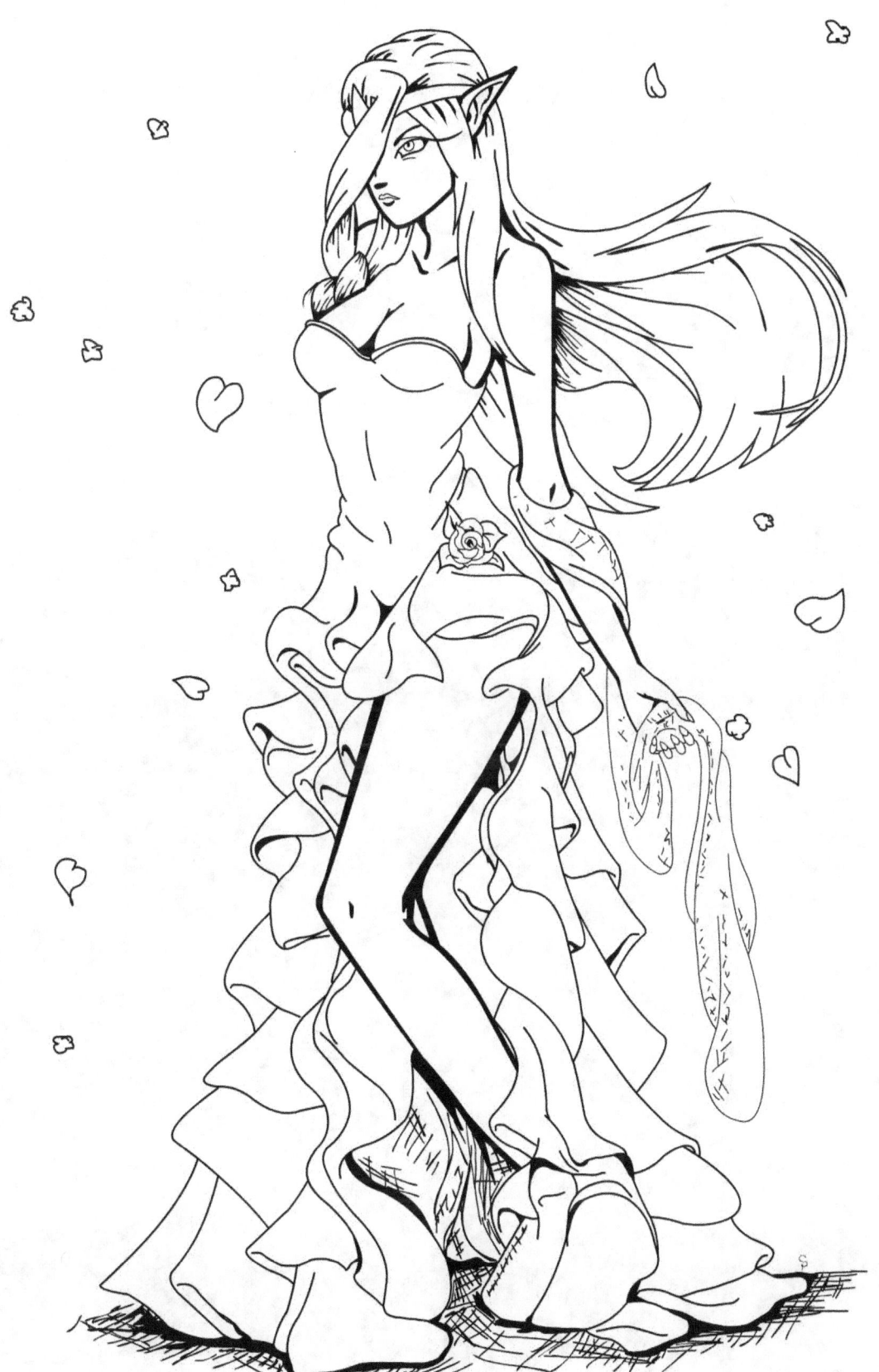

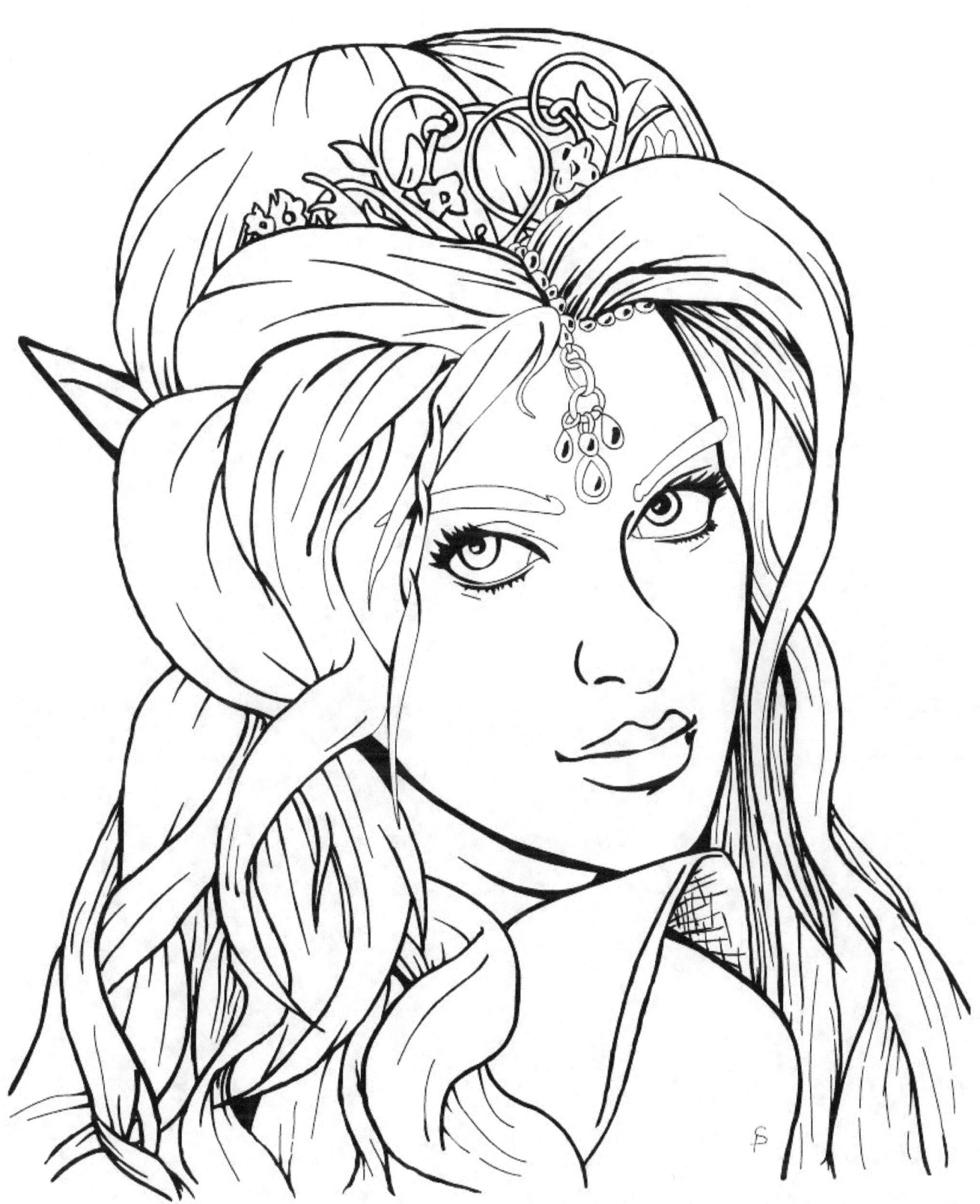

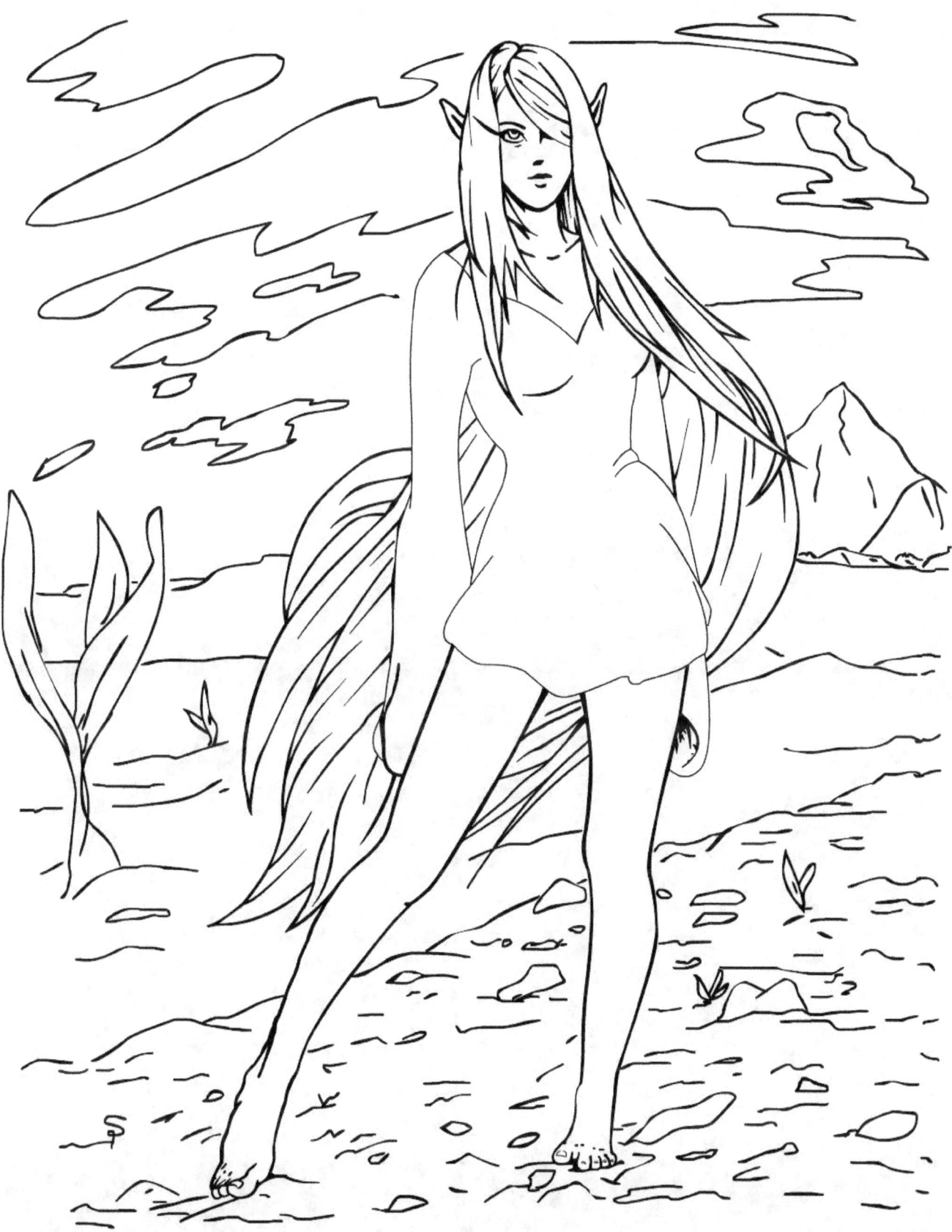

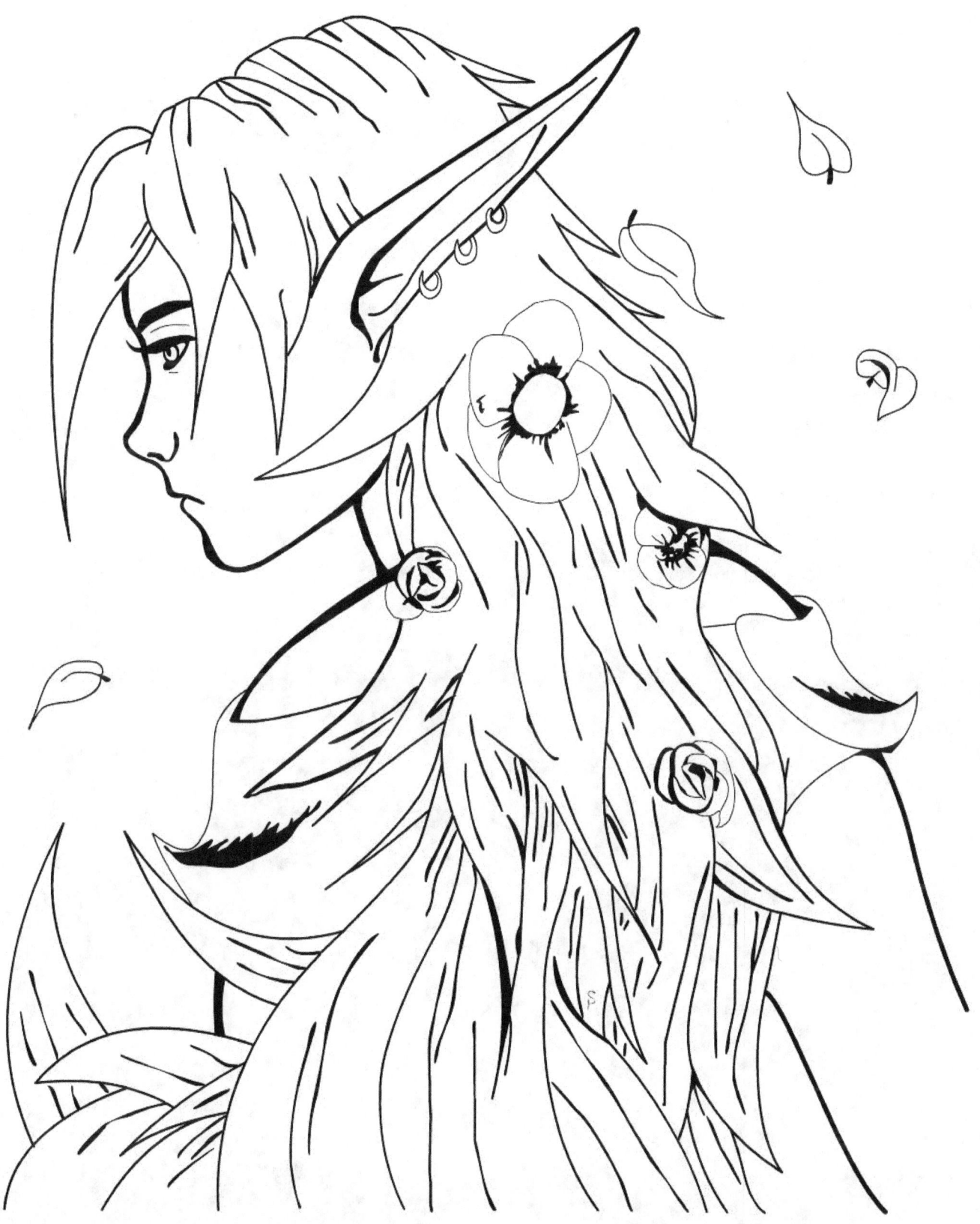

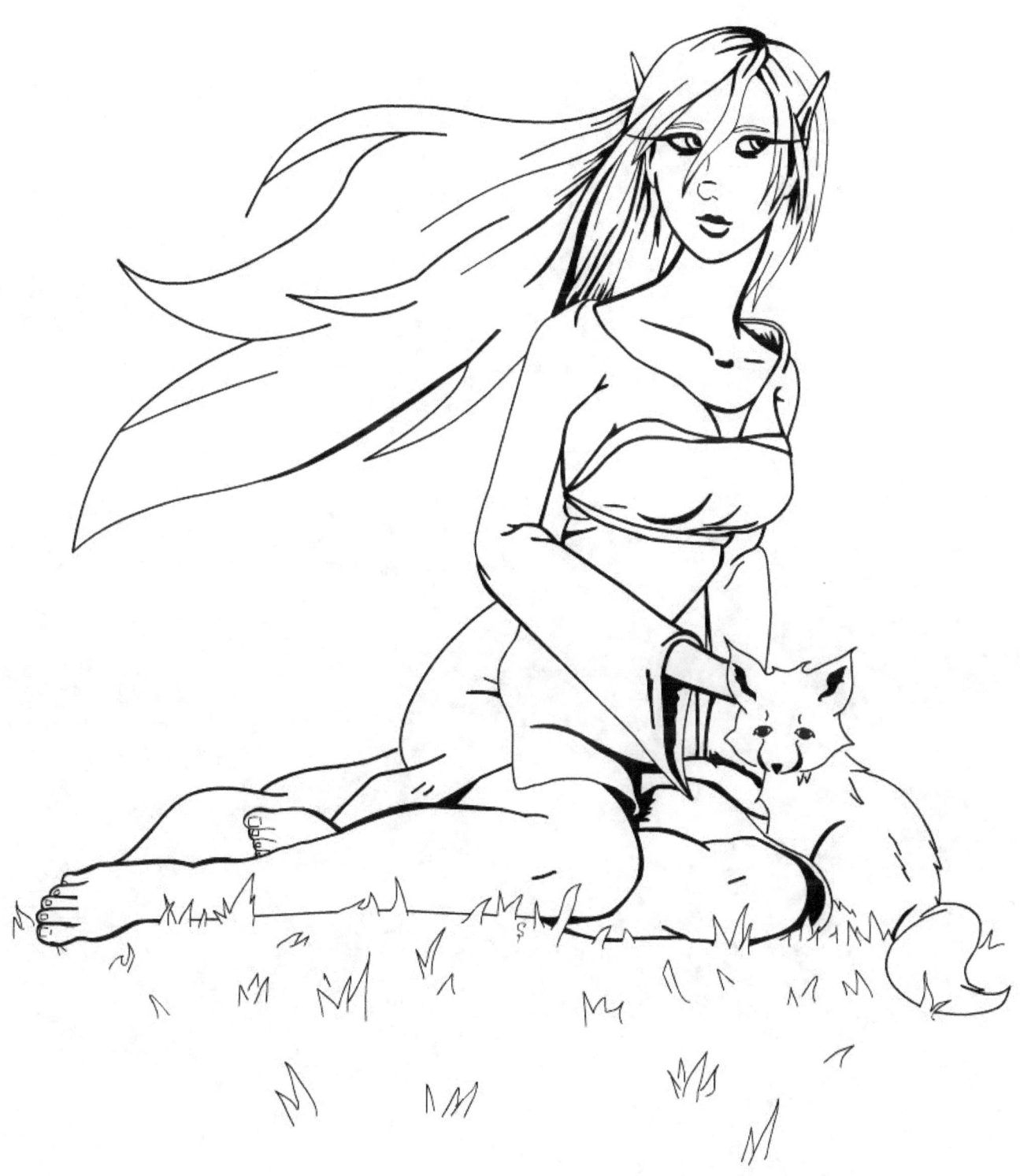

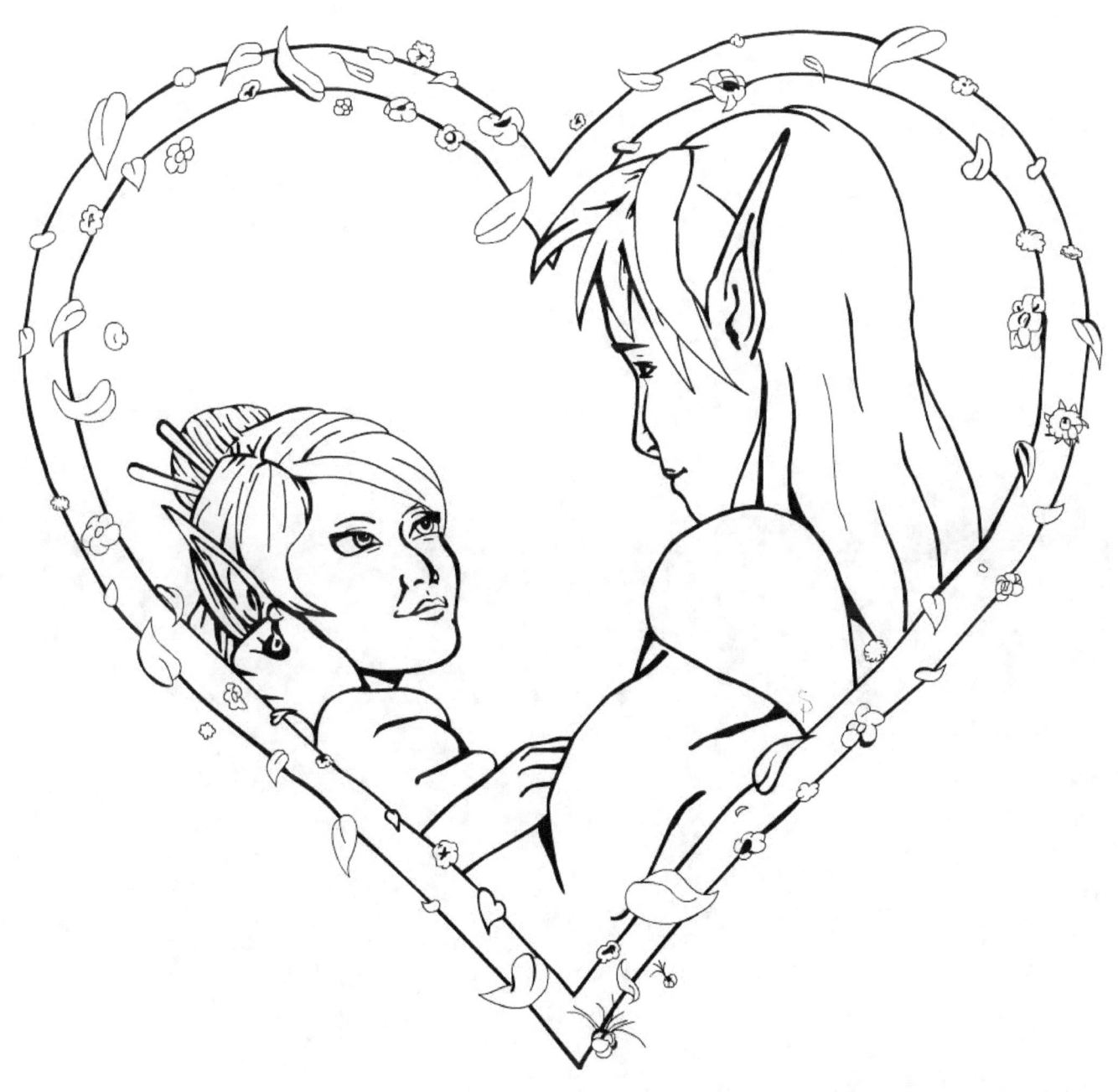

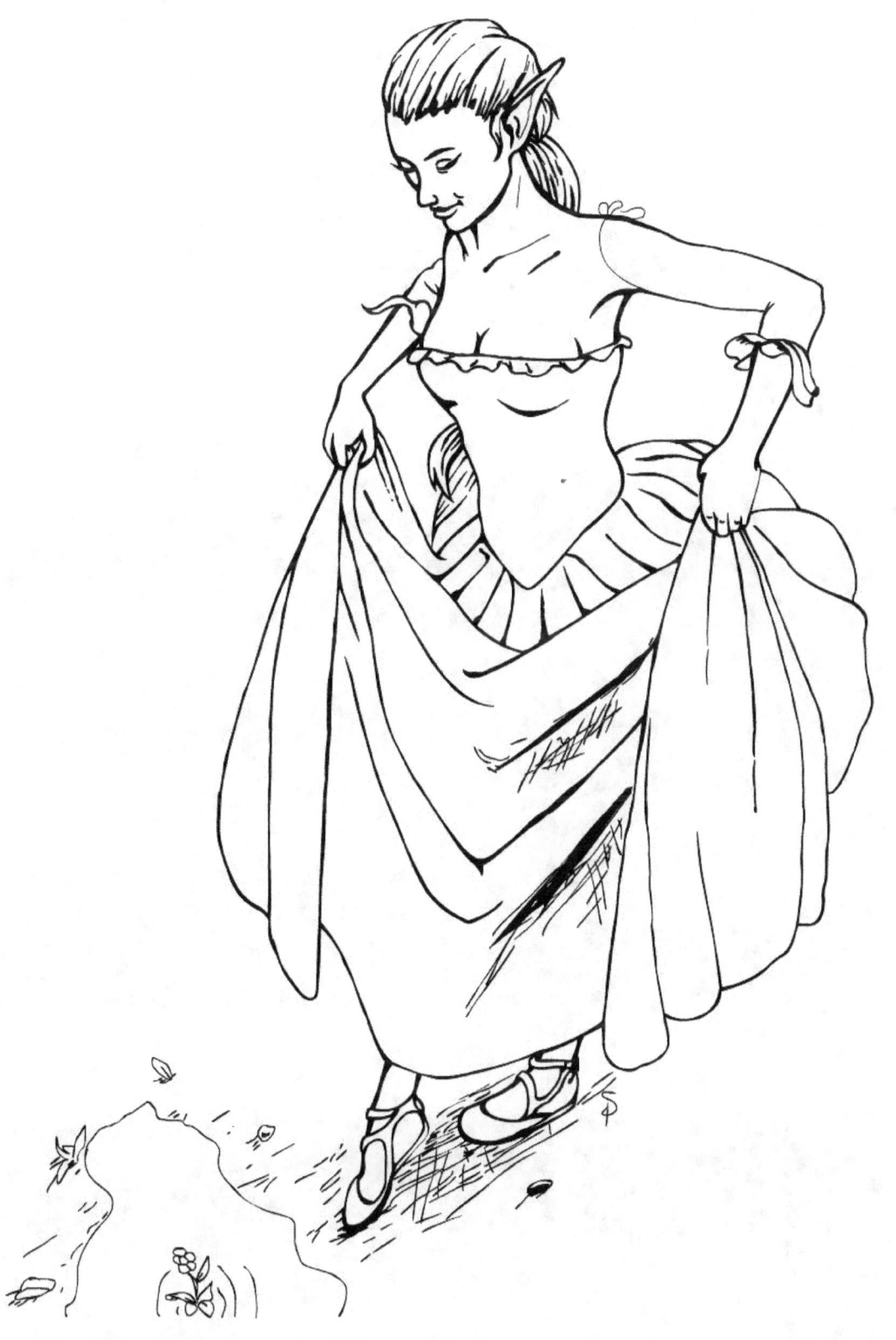

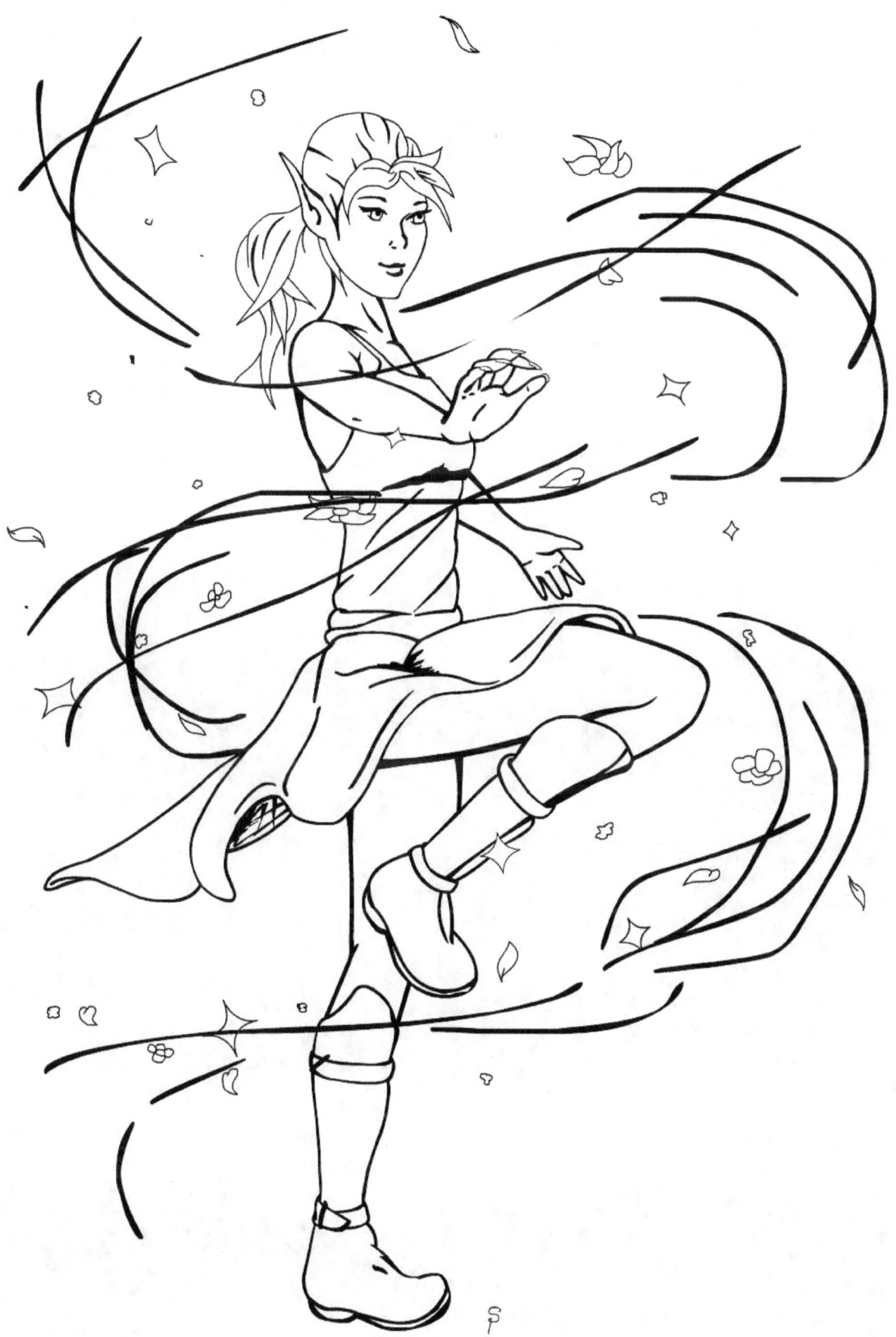

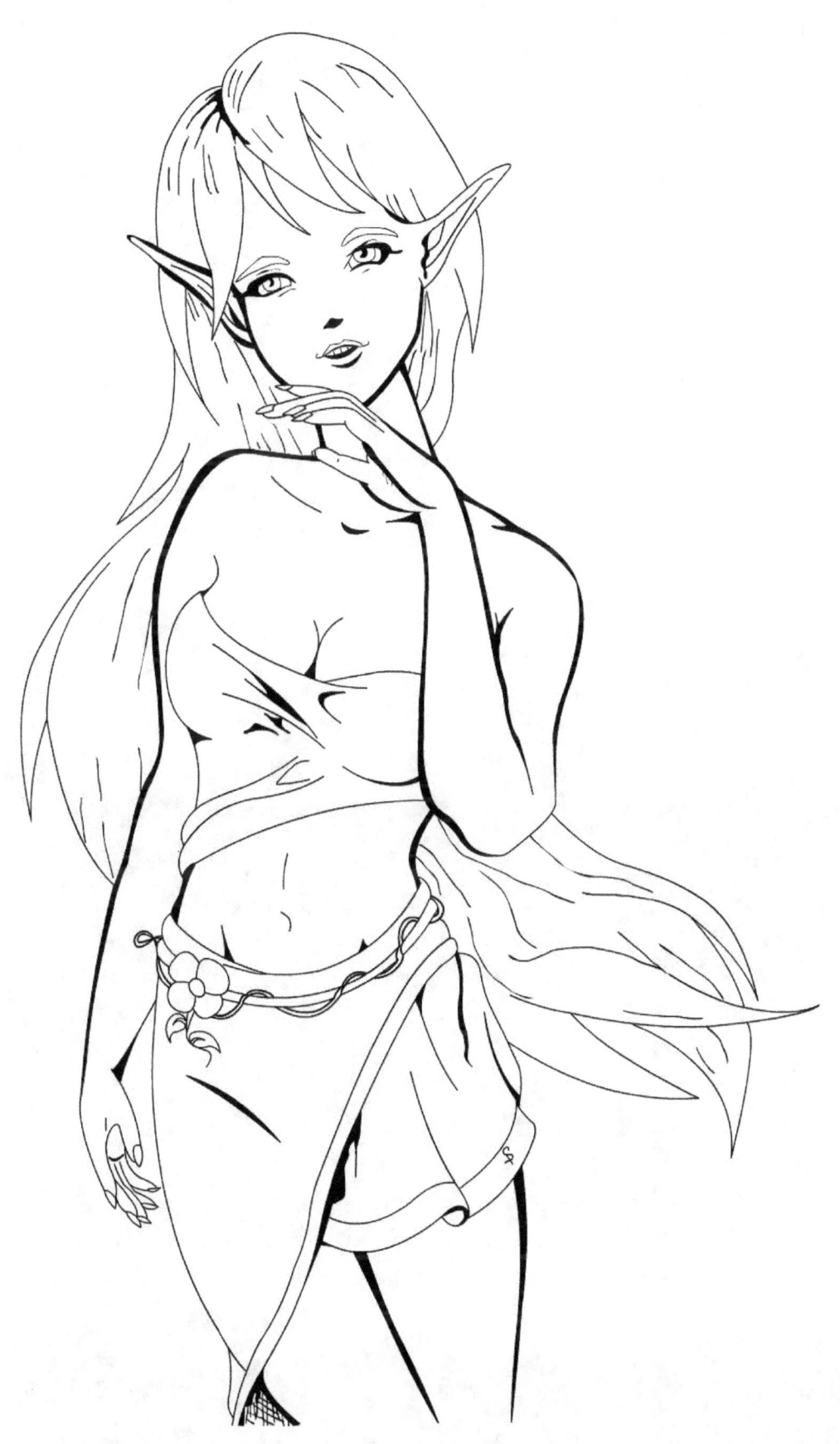

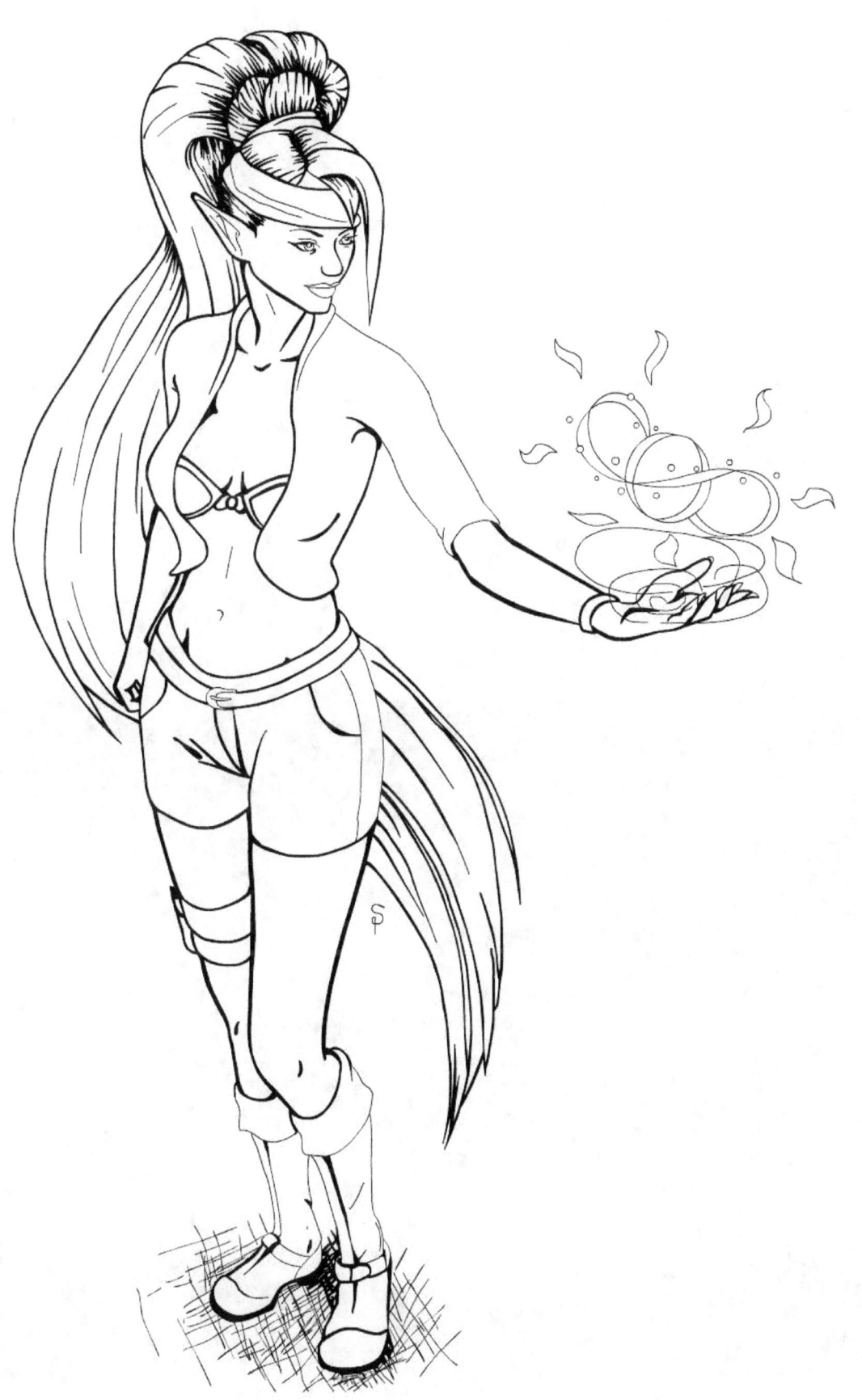

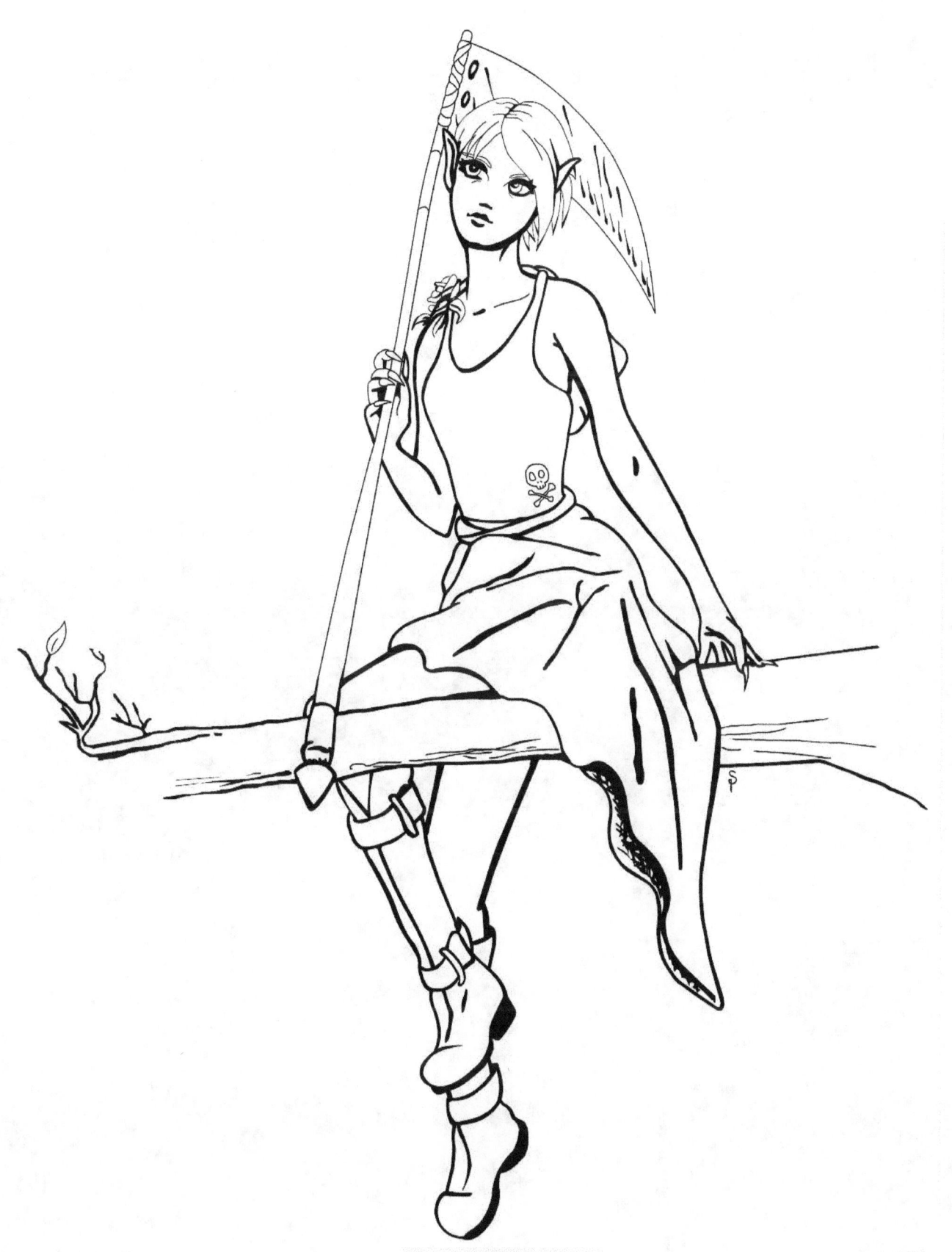

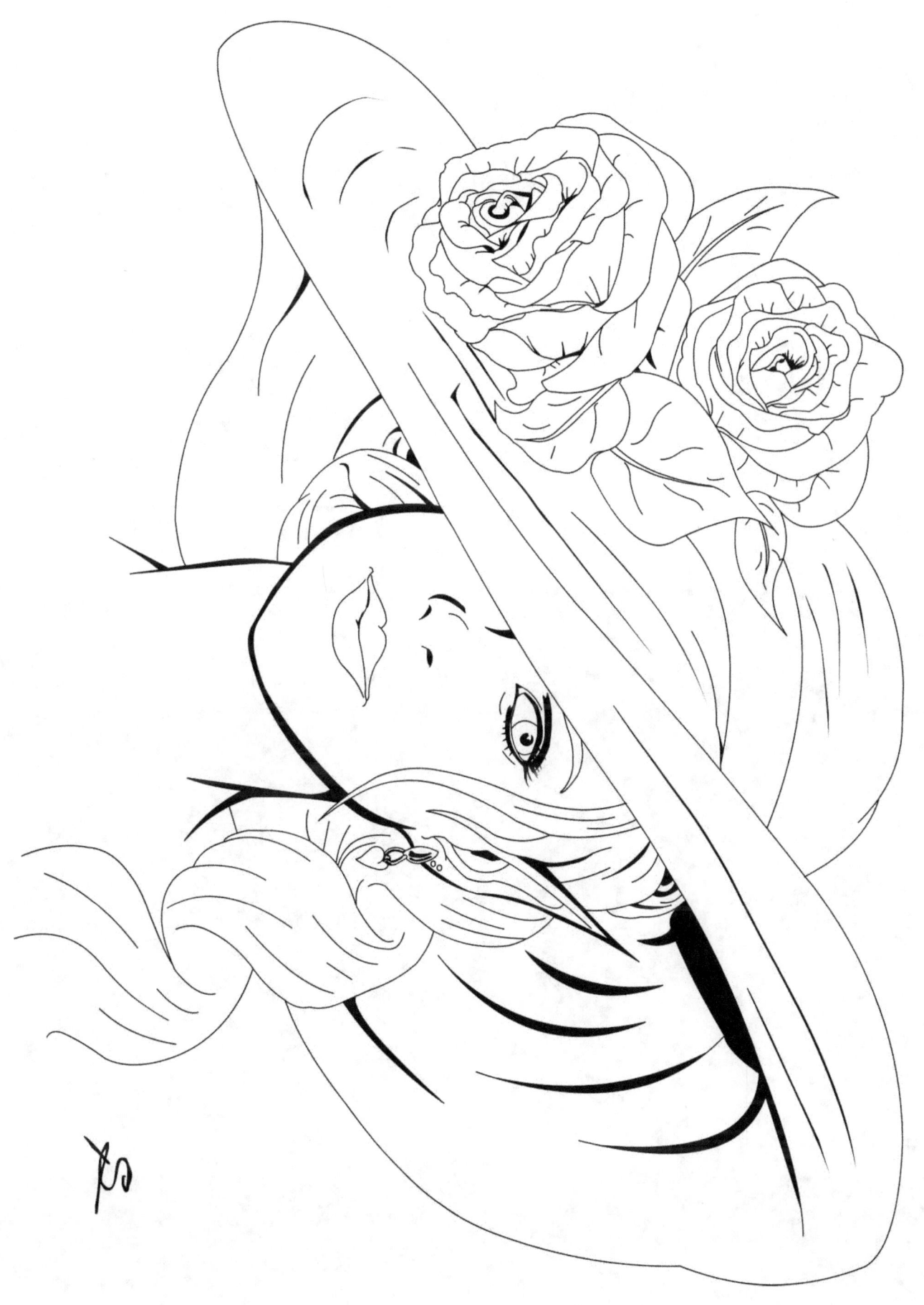

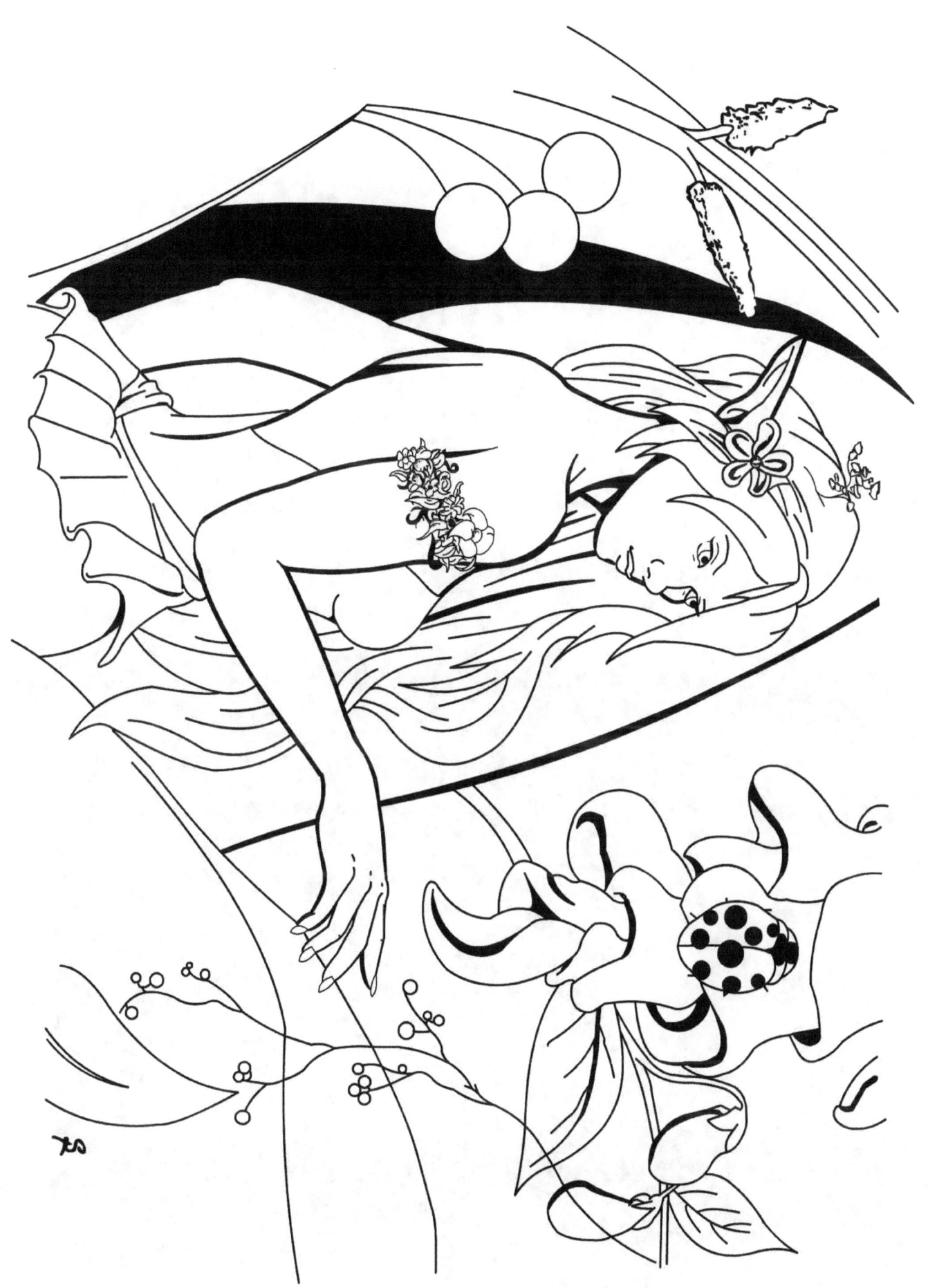

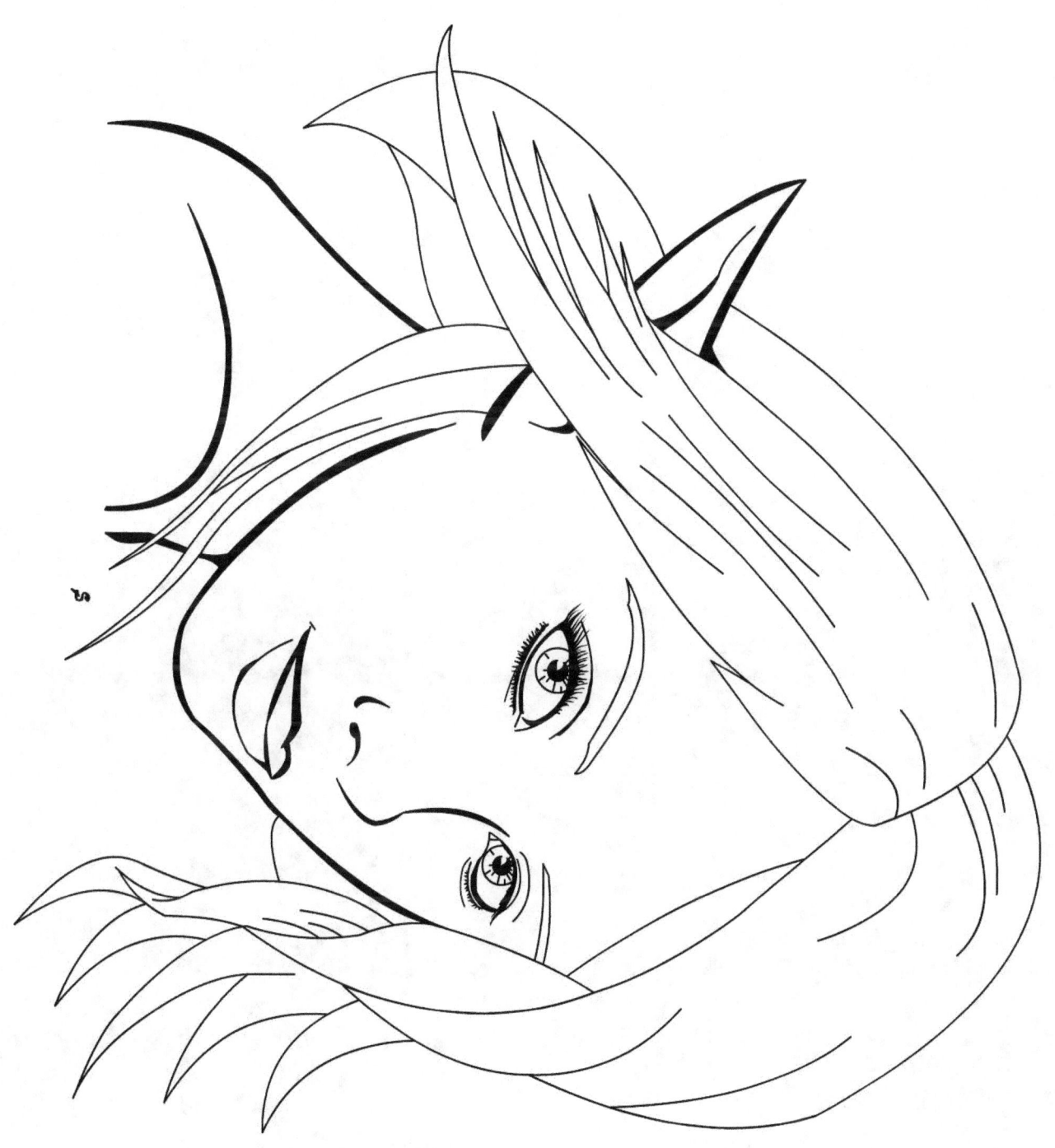

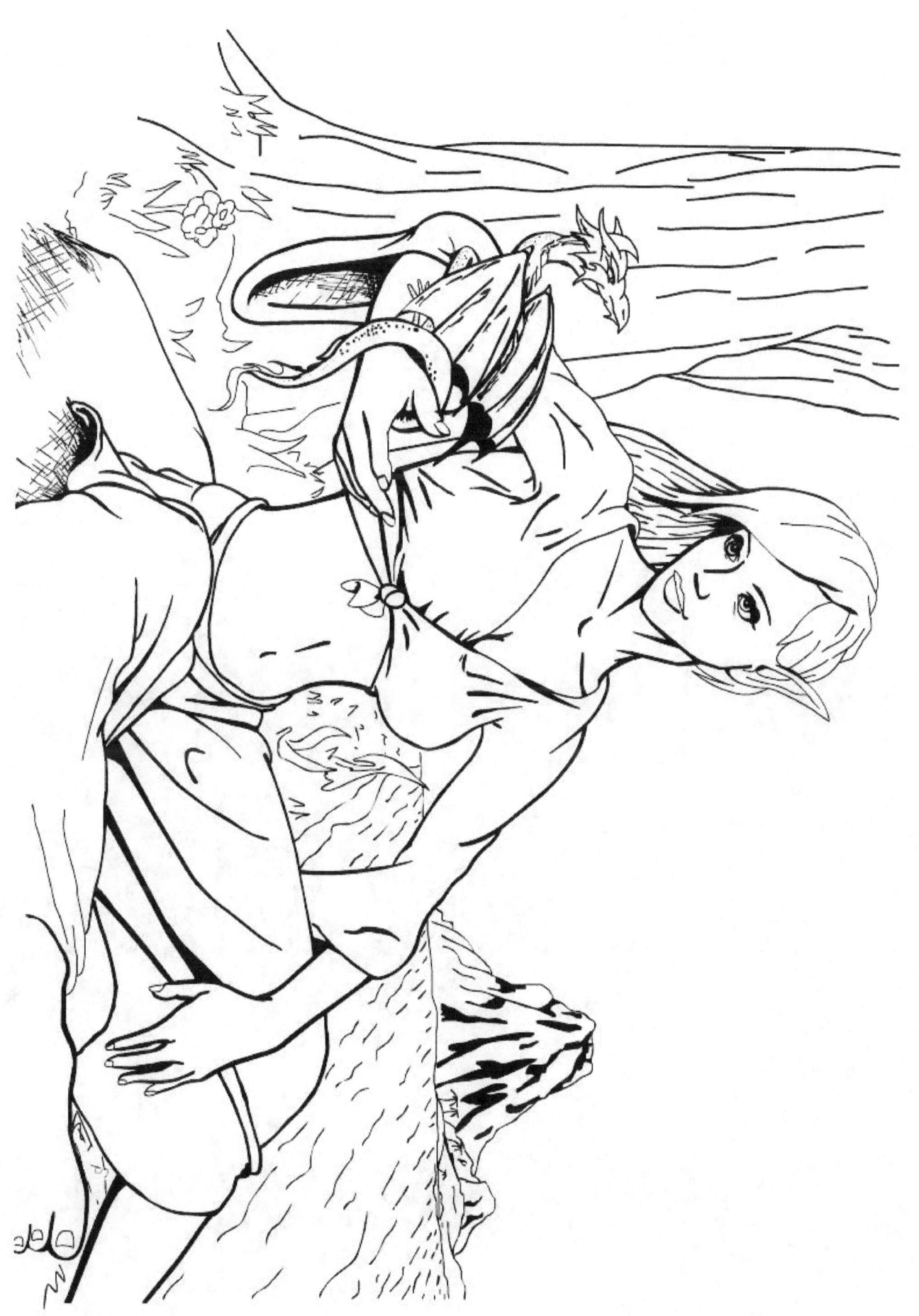

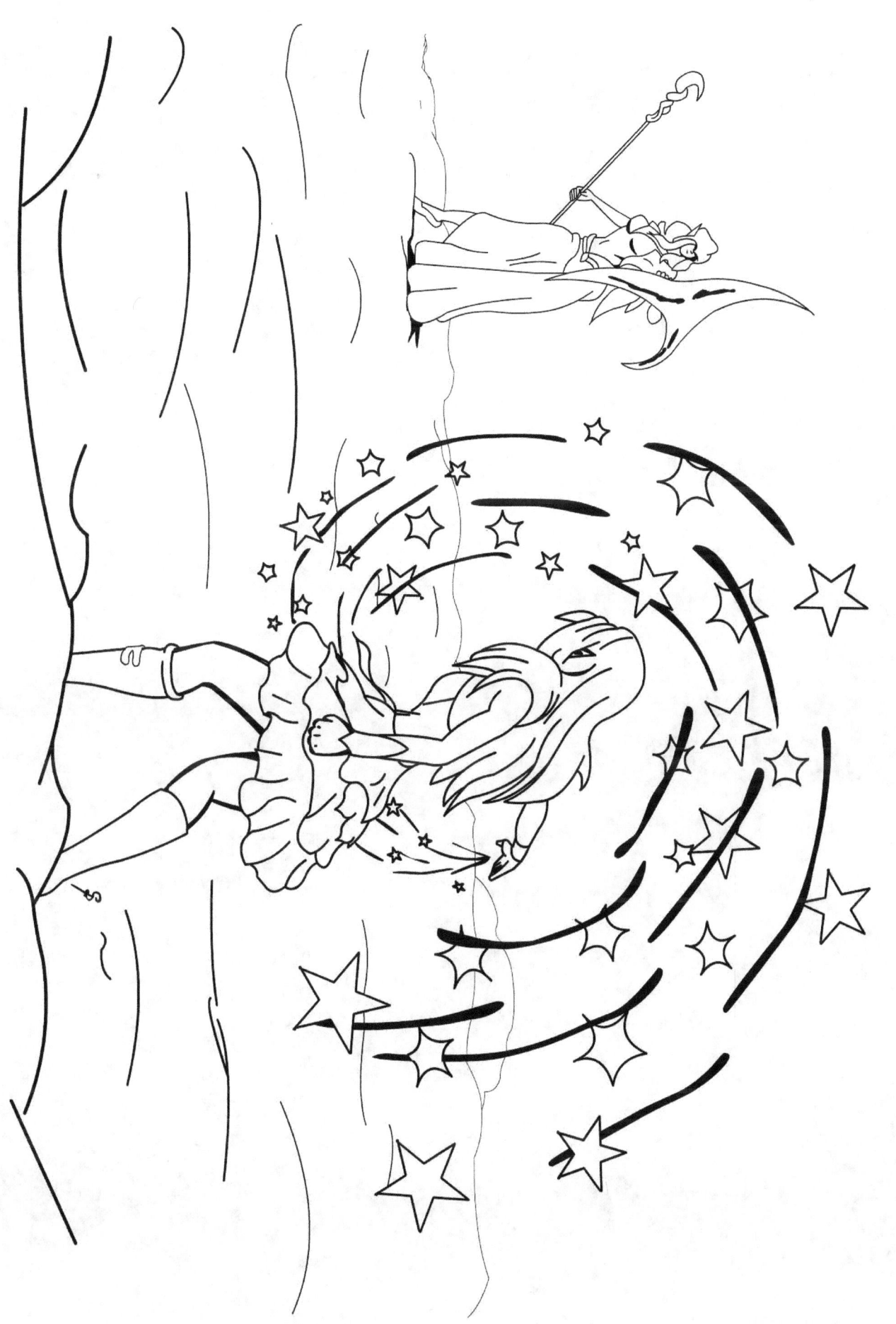

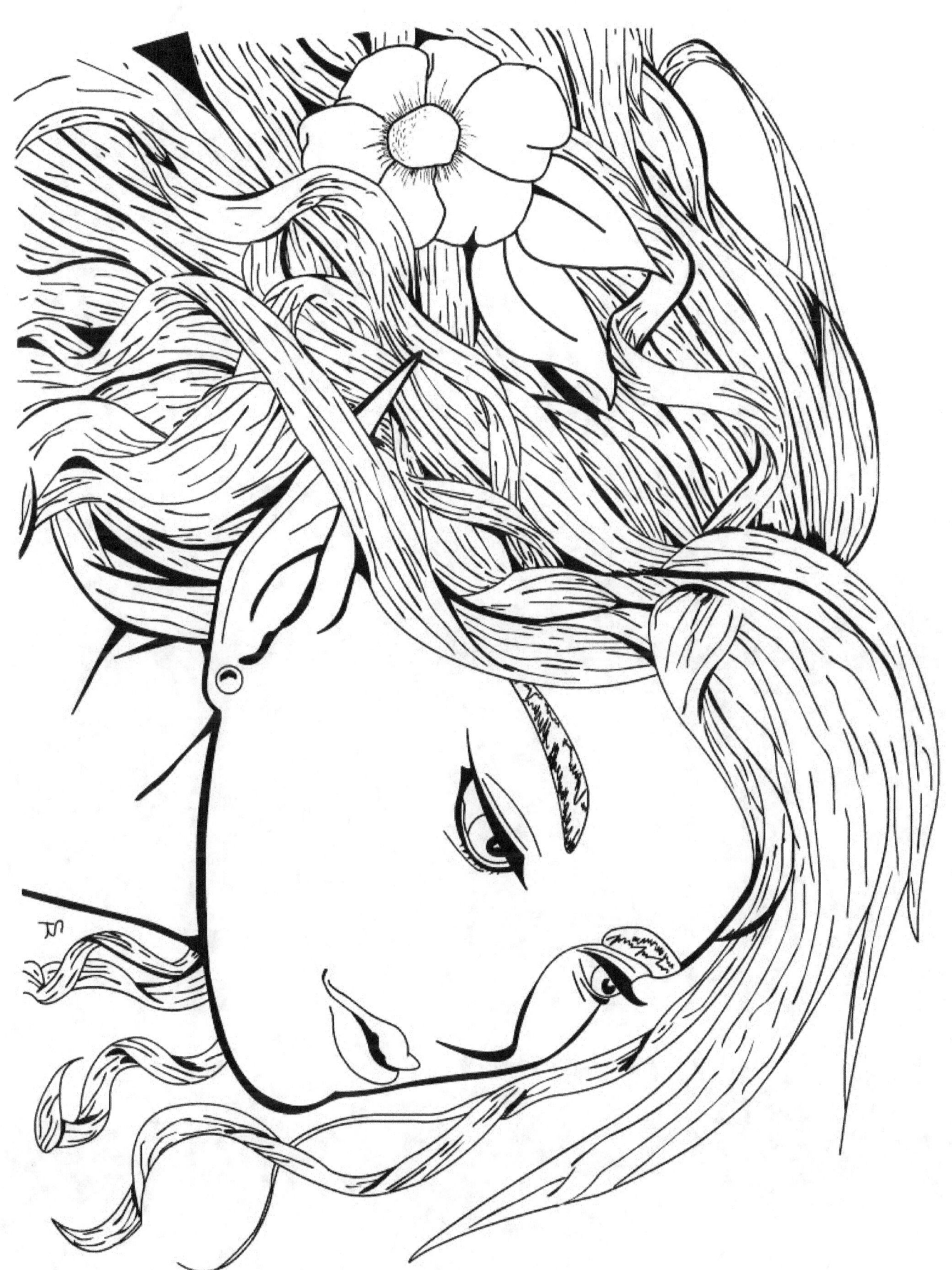

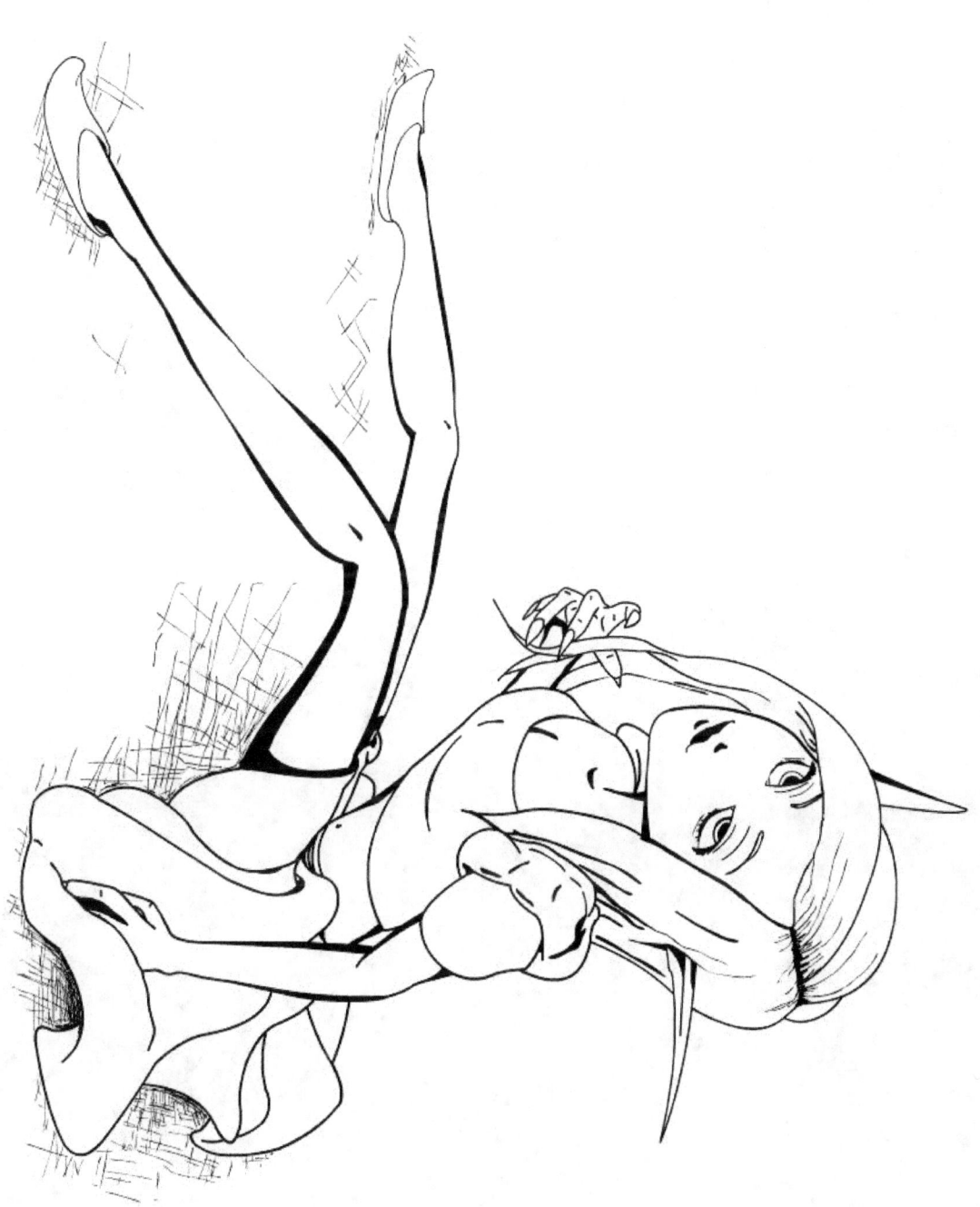

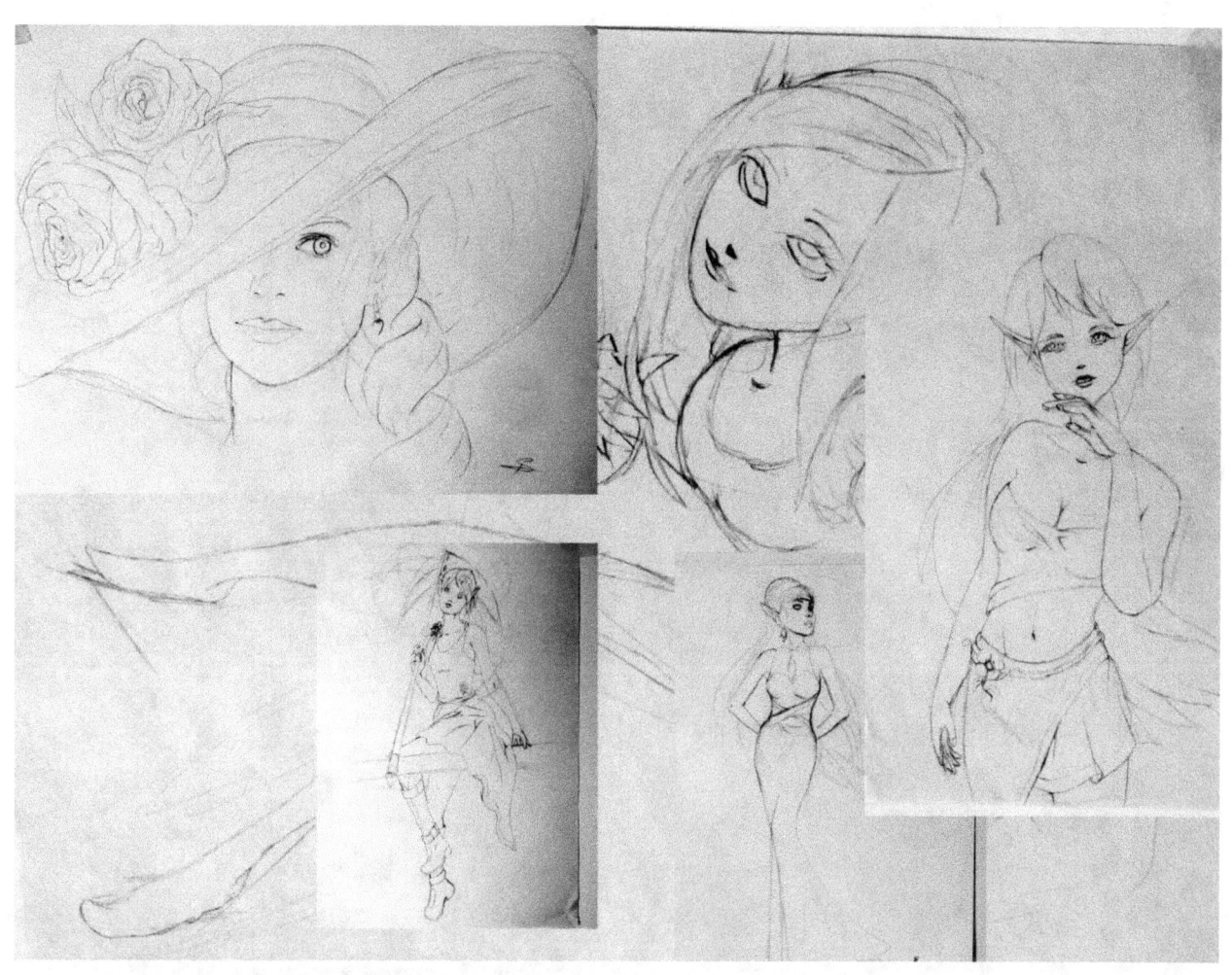

Thank you

Connect with my artist page at

www.facebook.com/cheetahryu

And look forward to my next edition: Beach Beauties.~ A day at the beach with crabs, sports, and fashionable swimwear.

www.ingramcontent.com/pod-product-compliance
Lightning Source LLC
Chambersburg PA
CBHW081357170526
45166CB00010B/3123